FORGIVENESS
The Freedom to Let Go

JUNE HUNT

AspirePress

Torrance, California

Forgiveness: The Freedom to Let Go
Copyright © 2013 Hope For The Heart
All rights reserved.
Aspire Press, a division of Rose Publishing, Inc.
4733 Torrance Blvd., #259
Torrance, California 90503 USA
www.aspirepress.com

Register your book at www.aspirepress.com/register
Get inspiration via email, sign up at www.aspirepress.com

Printed in the United States of America
040813DP

CONTENTS

Dear friend,

Have you ever had a serious struggle with forgiving someone? In the hidden recesses of your heart, have you wanted to see those who have wronged you receive severe judgment rather than forgiveness? If so, I understand.

I know all about harboring an unforgiving heart. For a number of years, I felt totally justified in harboring unforgiveness toward my father. He was an unbeliever who lived a lifestyle of infidelity.

At the same time, my mother was my "soft spot." If you had known her, you would wonder, *How could anyone want to hurt her?* She was compassionate, kind, and caring. Consequently, I would try to protect her from his cruel treatment … but no matter how hard I tried, I failed. The truth is, whenever she hurt, I hurt.

I remember how easy it was for me to focus on my father's faults! I would look for areas where he was wrong. Of course, since he never admitted to wrongdoing, I felt absolutely justified in my hatred. I would never have *called* it hatred. I didn't see myself in that light—as bitter. Why? Because the fact that I could still see his faults proved I was right.

I later became a Christian and learned about the forgiveness, mercy, and grace of God. Yet, I still felt justified in my hatred and unforgiveness. Why? Because my father had not changed. In order for me to forgive him, he had to change … that was my requirement.

I never will forget the day I came face-to-face with a passage that changed my perspective. It's found in 1 John 2:9–11: *"Whoever loves his brother lives in the light, and there is nothing in him to make him stumble. But whoever hates his brother is in the darkness and walks around in the darkness; he does not know where he is going, because the darkness has blinded him."*

I suddenly realized I had been blind to anything good that my father had done. All I could see or wanted to see was the negative. I remember asking my mother, "How can you be so nice to him?" Her answer was telling! "Oh, honey, if only he had the Lord, he wouldn't be that way." That was the key. She looked beyond his faults to see his need—He needed the Savior. She and her friends were praying for him to have a changed heart.

Six months before my father died, he was willing to pray a prayer of salvation. I am convinced that this occurred because my mother had nurtured the soil of his heart with compassion and forgiveness—the hardened ground had become soft—so that when the seed of truth was shared, it actually took root.

No matter what your circumstances, it's never too late to choose the road of forgiveness.

My hope is that through this book, God will speak to your heart and deepen your desire to walk the road of forgiveness every day of your life.

How I pray that you will experience the freedom that comes from embracing a heart of forgiveness!

Yours in the Lord's hope,

June

June Hunt

FORGIVENESS
The Freedom to Let Go

The year is 1944. Nazi Germany occupies Holland. An elderly watchmaker and his family are actively involved in the Dutch Underground. By hiding Jewish people in a secret room of their home, members of the Ten Boom family courageously help Jewish men, women, and children escape Hitler's roll call of death.[1]

Yet one fateful day, their secret is discovered. The watchmaker is arrested, and soon after being imprisoned, he dies. His tenderhearted daughter Betsie also cannot escape the jaws of death at the hands of her cruel captors. In the Nazi concentration camp, she perishes. And what about Corrie, the watchmaker's youngest daughter? Will she live … and, if so, will she ever be able to forgive her captors, those who caused the death of her father and her sister? While she is trying to survive the ravages of Ravensbruck, one of Hitler's most horrific death camps, can anything sustain Corrie ten Boom? To what can she cling? Indeed, Corrie does survive. Her God sustains her. She lives the truth of these words:

"False witnesses rise up against me, breathing out violence. I am still confident of this: I will see the goodness of the Lord in the land of the living. Wait for the Lord; be strong and take heart and wait for the Lord."
(Psalm 27:12–14)

DEFINITIONS

THE MANY FACES OF FORGIVENESS

Two years after the war, Corrie is speaking at a church in Munich. She has come from Holland to a defeated Germany, bringing with her the message that God does indeed forgive. There in the crowd, a solemn face stares back at her. As the people file out, a balding, heavyset man moves toward her—a man in a gray overcoat, a man clutching a brown felt hat. Suddenly a scene flashes back in her mind: *the blue uniform; the visored cap with its skull and crossbones; the huge room with its harsh, overhead lights; the humiliation of walking naked past this man …* this man who is now standing before her.

"You mentioned Ravensbruck in your talk. I was a guard there," he says. "But since that time I have become a Christian. I know that God has forgiven me for the cruel things I did there, but I would like to hear it from your lips as well."

He extends his hand toward her and asks, "Will you forgive me?"[2]

Corrie stares at the outstretched hand. The moment seems like hours as she wrestles with the most difficult decision she has ever had to make. Corrie knows Scripture well, but applying this passage seems to be too much:

"If your brother sins, rebuke him, and if he repents, forgive him. If he sins against you seven times in a day, and seven times comes back to you and says, 'I repent,' forgive him." (Luke 17:3–4)

WHAT IS Forgiveness?

Assume you need to borrow one hundred dollars to help pay a medical bill. You ask a friend for a loan and promise to pay it back at the end of the month. But when the time comes for repayment, you don't have the money. In fact, for the next three months, you still don't have the money. Then unexpectedly, out of the kindness of his heart, your friend *chooses* to "*forgive*" *the debt*! This is one facet of forgiveness.

> "Let no debt remain outstanding, except the continuing debt to love one another" (Romans 13:8).

▶ *Forgiveness* means dismissing a debt.[3]

In the New Testament, the Greek noun *aphesis* denotes a "dismissal" or "release."[4]

- When you *grant forgiveness*, you *dismiss* the debt owed to you.

- When you *receive forgiveness*, your debt is *dismissed*. (You are *released* from any requirement for repayment.)

- When you *grant forgiveness*, you *dismiss* the debt from your thoughts.

Jesus expressed the heart of forgiveness when He said, *"Love your enemies, do good to those who hate you"* (Luke 6:27).

▶ *Forgiveness* is dismissing your demand that others owe you something, especially when they fail to meet your expectations, fail to keep a promise, and fail to treat you justly.

Jesus said, *"If someone strikes you on the right cheek, turn to him the other also"* (Matthew 5:39).

▶ *Forgiveness* is dismissing, canceling, or setting someone free from the consequence of falling short of God's standard.

- The holy standard of God is perfection, yet we all have sinned.
- The penalty for our sins is spiritual death (separation from God).
- The penalty for our sins (our debt) was paid by Jesus through His sacrificial death on the cross. Therefore, instead of being separated from God, we can have our debt dismissed by God and experience eternal life in heaven.

"Everyone who believes in him [Jesus]
receives forgiveness of sins
through his name."
(Acts 10:43)

QUESTION: "Is it possible to sin beyond God's ability to forgive?"

ANSWER: No. God promises to purify us from *all* unrighteousness, not just specific sins, but we need to first confess our sins. (*Confess* means literally "to agree"—to agree with God.)[5] And if we agree with God about our sin, we not only admit we have sinned, but we also turn from our sins and turn to Jesus, entrusting our lives to the One who died for our sins.

> "I acknowledged my sin to you and did not cover up my iniquity. I said, 'I will confess my transgressions to the LORD'—and you forgave the guilt of my sin."
> (Psalm 32:5)

Misconceptions abound when the word *forgiveness* is mentioned. Some think forgiveness is the equivalent of *excusing* sin, saying that what was wrong is now right. Yet this is not the example of forgiveness that Jesus displayed. When He encountered the mob of men eager to stone a woman caught in adultery, He chose not to stone her; however, never did He *excuse* her. Instead, He said, *"Go, and sin no more"* (John 8:11 KJV). To help correct any confusion, you need to know *what forgiveness is not*!

▶ *Forgiveness is not* circumventing God's justice.

It is allowing God to execute His justice in His time and in His way.

▶ *Forgiveness is not* waiting for "time to heal all wounds."

It is clear that time doesn't heal wounds—some people will not allow healing.

▶ *Forgiveness is not* letting the guilty "off the hook."

It is moving the guilty from your hook to God's hook.

▶ *Forgiveness is not* the same as reconciliation.

It takes two for reconciliation, only one for forgiveness.

▶ *Forgiveness is not* excusing unjust behavior.

It is acknowledging that unjust behavior is without excuse, while still forgiving.

► *Forgiveness is not* explaining away the hurt.

It is working through the hurt.

► *Forgiveness is not* based on what is fair.

It was not "fair" for Jesus to hang on the cross—but He did so that we could be forgiven.

► *Forgiveness is not* being a weak martyr.

It is being strong enough to be Christlike.

► *Forgiveness is not* stuffing your anger.

It is resolving your anger by releasing the offense to God.

► *Forgiveness is not* a natural response.

It is a supernatural response, empowered by God.

► *Forgiveness is not* denying the hurt.

It is feeling the hurt and releasing it.

► *Forgiveness is not* being a doormat.

It is seeing that, if this were so, Jesus would have been the greatest doormat of all!

► *Forgiveness is not* conditional.

It is unconditional, a mandate from God to everyone.

► *Forgiveness is not* forgetting.

It is necessary to remember before you can forgive.

► *Forgiveness is not* a feeling.

It is a choice—an act of the will.

"Let the wise listen and add to their learning, and let the discerning get guidance." (Proverbs 1:5)

Biblical Example

A loose woman was caught "in the act," and the stone throwers were ready. The penalty for adultery was clear—*stone the adulterers to death!* Jesus challenged the stone throwers to examine their own hearts before condemning the woman's behavior. "The one who is without sin—you cast the first stone." No one moved. Then, after all the stones dropped—one by one—and the stone throwers left—one by one—Jesus focused His attention on the woman. He looked beyond her fault and saw her need. She needed to know the life-changing love of God. Unexpectedly, Jesus gave her a priceless gift—His merciful favor and forgiveness. (See John 8:3–11.)

> "'Neither do I condemn you,'
> Jesus declared. 'Go now and
> leave your life of sin.'"
> (John 8:11)

QUESTION: "If I don't feel like forgiving, how can I be asked to forgive? That doesn't seem right."

ANSWER: Forgiveness is not based on a *feeling*, but rather on the *fact* that we—all of us—are called by God to forgive. Forgiveness is not an *emotion*, but is rather an act of the *will*. Therefore, what "seems right" based on feelings can easily be wrong!

> "There is a way that seems right to a man,
> but in the end it leads to death."
> (Proverbs 14:12)

Imagine that you are a runner and the race is an event in the Olympics. You have the right shoes, right shorts, right shirt. Yet, something is desperately wrong. Locked on your ankle is a heavy, black ball and chain! This weight is too heavy—you can't run the distance—you can't even qualify. If only you could figure out a way to free yourself, but you don't have the key to unlock the chain.

Then, on the day of the qualifying run, you are told that you already possess the key to freedom. Quickly, you free yourself, and, oh, what freedom! It is as though that black ball miraculously turns into a big helium balloon. The load is lifted. The balloon is released. The weight is "sent away."

Previously, no one had told you that your unforgiveness was the black ball weighing you down. Now that you know that forgiveness is one of the major keys to freedom, you can run the race and cross the finish line with freedom.

> **"Let us throw off everything that hinders and the sin that so easily entangles, and let us run with perseverance the race marked out for us."**
> **(Hebrews 12:1)**

▶ **To forgive** means to *release your resentment* toward your offender.

In the New Testament, the Greek verb **aphiemi** primarily means "to send away"—in other words, "to *forgive*, send away or release the penalty when someone wrongs you."[7] This implies that you need …

- *To release* your right to hear "I'm sorry"
- *To release* your right to be bitter
- *To release* your right to get even

"Do not repay anyone evil for evil. Be careful to do what is right in the eyes of everybody."
(Romans 12:17)

▶ **To forgive** is to *release your rights* regarding the offense.

- *To release* your right to dwell on the offense
- *To release* your right to hold on to the offense
- *To release* your right to keep bringing up the offense

"He who covers over an offense promotes love, but whoever repeats the matter separates close friends."
(Proverbs 17:9)

▶ **To forgive** is to *reflect the character of Christ.* Just as God is willing to forgive us, we are called to forgive others.

- *To forgive* is to extend mercy.
- *To forgive* is to give a gift of grace.
- *To forgive* is to set the offender free.

Jesus taught his disciples to pray,

> "Forgive us our debts, as we also have forgiven our debtors." (Matthew 6:12)

QUESTION: "What can I do when I don't feel like forgiving?"

ANSWER: Whenever you don't feel like doing something you should do, examine your thoughts. While you can't control what your offenders do, you can control your thinking about your offenders. God gives us much counsel about what we should sift out from our thinking. Imagine that the Bible is a "thought-sifter"—a tool that helps us sift the thoughts that should not go into our minds. Evaluate your thoughts about those who offend you. Remember: Your thoughts produce your feelings. Do your thoughts naturally flow through "the thought-sifter" in Scripture below? If not, catch them before they pass through and sift them out! When you carefully choose what you will dwell on, your emotions will begin to line up, and you will gradually even feel like forgiving.

> "Whatever is true, whatever is noble, whatever is right, whatever is pure, whatever is lovely, whatever is admirable—if anything is excellent or praiseworthy—think about such things." (Philippians 4:8)

No. Forgiveness is not the same as reconciliation. Forgiveness focuses on the offense, whereas reconciliation focuses on the relationship. Forgiveness requires no relationship. However, reconciliation requires a relationship in which two people, in agreement, are walking together toward the same goal. The Bible says, *"Do two walk together unless they have agreed to do so?"* (Amos 3:3)

▶ *Forgiveness* can take place with only one person.

Reconciliation requires at least two persons.

▶ *Forgiveness* is directed one-way.

Reconciliation is reciprocal, occurring two-ways.

▶ *Forgiveness* is a decision to release the offender.

Reconciliation is the effort to rejoin the offender.

▶ *Forgiveness* involves a change in thinking about the offender.

Reconciliation involves a change in behavior by the offender.

▶ *Forgiveness* is a free gift to the one who has broken trust.

Reconciliation is a restored relationship based on restored trust.

▶ *Forgiveness* is extended even if it is never, ever earned.

Reconciliation is offered to the offender because it has been earned.

▶ *Forgiveness* is unconditional, regardless of a lack of repentance.

Reconciliation is conditional, based on repentance.

QUESTION: **"After we forgive someone, must we also *try* to be reconciled?"**

ANSWER: The answer to this question is sometimes *yes* and sometimes *no*.

▶ Most of the time God's desire for us is reconciliation. Second Corinthians 5:18 says, *"God ... reconciled us to himself through Christ and gave us the ministry of reconciliation."*

▶ However, sometimes encouraging the restoration of a relationship is not at all wise, as with a partner in adultery or with a rapist. First Corinthians 15:33 says, *"Do not be misled: 'Bad company corrupts good character.'"* For instance, if a husband's anger is out of control and he refuses to get help for his violent temper, the wife needs to take this Scripture to heart and move out of harm's way until counseling and lasting changes are a part of his lifestyle.

"Do not make friends with a hot-tempered man, do not associate with one easily angered." (Proverbs 22:24)

Do you sometimes struggle with forgiving others? Understand that your awareness of how much God loves you and continually forgives you can be the catalyst to compel you to forgive others. Then you can actually forgive others with the Lord's "divine forgiveness." *"The Lord our God is merciful and forgiving, even though we have rebelled against him."* (Daniel 9:9)

▶ ***Divine forgiveness*** is the fact that God, in His mercy, chose to release you from the penalty for your sins. (Unfortunately, some people refuse to receive this gift from God.)

"The LORD is compassionate and gracious, slow to anger, abounding in love. … He does not treat us as our sins deserve or repay us according to our iniquities. … As far as the east is from the west, so far has he removed our transgressions from us." (Psalm 103:8, 10, 12)

▶ ***Divine forgiveness*** was extended by Jesus, who paid the penalty for our sins in full—He died on the cross as payment for the sins of all people. While we owed a debt we could not pay, He paid a debt He did not owe.

One of the many Messianic prophecies states, *"We all, like sheep, have gone astray, each of us has turned to his own way; and the LORD has laid on him [Christ, the Messiah] the iniquity of us all"* (Isaiah 53:6).

▶ *Divine forgiveness* is an extension of grace as seen in the Greek word *charizomai*, which is translated "forgive" and means "to bestow a favor unconditionally."[9] The Greek word *charis* means "grace."[10] You are an expression of God's grace when you forgive others with divine forgiveness.

"Be kind and compassionate to one another, forgiving each other, just as in Christ God forgave you." (Ephesians 4:32)

Biblical Example

Joseph and His Brothers[11]

What could erupt in more resentment than friction within the family?

Joseph is a prime example of someone who could have chosen to be vindictive, rather than forgiving. (See Genesis chapters 37–45.) He is the favorite son of his father, Jacob. Joseph's ten older brothers are so bitter and jealous that they sell him into slavery. Later, he is falsely accused of attempted rape, unjustly imprisoned, and forgotten by a friend who promised to help. Joseph has every reason to sever ties with his family, vent hatred on humanity, and slam the door on God, but he doesn't.[12]

Later when Joseph becomes the prime minister of Egypt, severe famine plagues the land. But through God's involvement with Joseph, Egypt is well prepared. When his brothers hear of Egypt's abundance, they make a long journey from Canaan in order to obtain food. While in Egypt they encounter their brother Joseph, who they had thought was dead but has now become the prime minister! What an opportunity for Joseph to take revenge! But instead of settling the score, Joseph speaks kindly to them and recounts the way God used their treatment of him for his good, for their good, and for the good of the Jewish people.

> "Do not be distressed and do not be angry
> with yourselves for selling me here,
> because it was to save lives
> that God sent me ahead of you. ...
> To preserve for you a remnant on earth and
> to save your lives by a great deliverance. ...
> He made me father to Pharaoh,
> lord of his entire household
> and ruler of all Egypt."
> (Genesis 45:5–8)

Even though Joseph had been tossed into the deepest of pits, he emerged with extraordinary forgiveness toward those who wronged him. What was his secret?

The Secret to Joseph's Success

▶ *"Do not be distressed and do not be angry."*

When you realize that God, in His sovereignty, will bring good out of the *wrongs* done to you, you will have an attitude of forgiveness.

▶ *"God sent me."*

When you realize that God, in His sovereignty, will use your location (wherever you are placed) for good, you will have an attitude of forgiveness.

▶ *"He made me."*

When you realize that God, in His sovereignty, will make your every circumstance result in good, you will have an attitude of forgiveness.

▶ *Conclusion*

When you are able to accept God's sovereignty over your location, your circumstances, and especially the wrongs done to you, and when you trust Him to use them one day for good … you will have success through your forgiveness!

"We know that in all things God works for the good of those who love him, who have been called according to his purpose." (Romans 8:28)

QUESTION: "How can I respond in a Christlike way when I'm being treated so unjustly?"[13]

ANSWER: Realize that Christ suffered unjustly and horrendously to pay the penalty for your sins—to make possible forgiveness of your sins. Therefore, after you become a true Christian, you rely on Christ (who lives in you) to enable you to endure your unjust suffering—but even more so, to forgive those who mistreat you. Be clear about this point: every authentic Christian is "called" to suffer, but with that suffering comes a blessing.

"It is commendable if a man bears up
under the pain of unjust suffering
because he is conscious of God. ...
To this you were called, because
Christ suffered for you,
leaving you an example, that you should
follow in his steps. 'He committed no sin,
and no deceit was found in his mouth.'
When they hurled their insults at him,
he did not retaliate; when he suffered,
he made no threats. Instead, he entrusted
himself to him who judges justly."
(1 Peter 2:19–23)

CHARACTERISTICS OF UNFORGIVENESS

Here stands the enemy, the former Nazi SS officer. His very presence stands for cruelty and the stench of crematoriums at Ravensbruck. As Corrie ten Boom stares at the rough hand offered by her former captor, she knows in her head what she has to do—*forgive*! But her emotions scream silently in opposition. The very message she has been sharing with the victims of Nazi brutality emphasizes that she must forgive those who persecuted her. Forgiveness is a necessity. But Corrie stands paralyzed as the battle rages between her mind and her emotions.

And I stood there—I whose sins had again and again to be forgiven—and could not forgive. [My sister] Betsie had died in that place—could he erase her slow terrible death simply for the asking?[14]

Imagine Corrie's dilemma. She knows that those who have forgiven their enemies have also been able to rebuild their lives regardless of the physical horrors they suffered. But those who continue to nurse their bitterness remain imprisoned, not in Hitler's horrid concentration camps, but within their own wounded souls. Corrie knows the cost of bitterness—the very bitterness she is battling—because the Bible says, *"See to it that no one misses the grace of God and that no bitter root grows up to cause trouble and defile many."* (Hebrews 12:15)

When you refuse to forgive, your unforgiveness keeps you *emotionally stuck to both the offense and the offender*. A *continual* refusal to forgive digs a deeper hole in which you can easily hide your hardened heart.

Blaming others is a favorite tactic to justify unforgiveness. You can become too comfortable in the unnatural habitat of self-righteousness and self-pity. Your past hurts, though buried, are still very much alive. And because they are not released in God's way, oddly enough, you *become like your offender* (but you are blind to it). Not forgiving your offender is an offense to God, thereby making you an offender to God as well! The Bible says to confess and renounce this sin.

> **"He who conceals his sins does not prosper, but whoever confesses and renounces them finds mercy."**
> **(Proverbs 28:13)**

THE UNFORGIVING HEART IS ...

Judgmental—focusing on the past wrongs that the offender committed.

THE UNFORGIVING HEART HAS ...

Condemnation—being intolerant of any present failures of the offender.

"Do not judge . ... Do not condemn . ...
Forgive, and you will be forgiven."
(Luke 6:37)

THE UNFORGIVING HEART IS ...

Merciless—rehearsing the reasons why the offender does not deserve mercy.

THE UNFORGIVING HEART HAS ...

Contempt—looking down without mercy on the offender.

"Judgment without mercy will be shown to
anyone who has not been merciful.
Mercy triumphs over judgment!"
(James 2:13)

THE UNFORGIVING HEART IS ...

Resentful—begrudging the successes of the offender.

THE UNFORGIVING HEART HAS ...

Envy—coveting the accomplishments of the offender.

"Resentment kills a fool,
and envy slays the simple."
(Job 5:2)

The Unforgiving Heart Is ...

Vengeful—rejoicing when the offender experiences failure, difficulty, or hurt.

The Unforgiving Heart Has ...

Retaliation—desiring to get even with the offender.

"Do not gloat when your enemy falls; when he stumbles, do not let your heart rejoice." (Proverbs 24:17)

The Unforgiving Heart Is ...

Maligning—talking to others about the faults of the offender with the intent to hurt.

The Unforgiving Heart Has ...

Slander—sharing unnecessary negatives about the offender.

"He who conceals his hatred has lying lips, and whoever spreads slander is a fool." (Proverbs 10:18)

The Unforgiving Heart Is ...

Prideful—elevating self above the offender, who is considered less deserving.

The Unforgiving Heart Has ...

Haughtiness—acting with arrogance toward the offender.

"Pride goes before destruction, a haughty spirit before a fall." (Proverbs 16:18)

THE UNFORGIVING HEART IS ...

Profane—verbally abusive toward the offender.

THE UNFORGIVING HEART HAS ...

Bitterness—harboring hostility toward the offender.

> "Their mouths are full of cursing
> and bitterness."
> (Romans 3:14)

THE UNFORGIVING HEART IS ...

Complaining—and quick to quarrel over personal choices, words, and deeds.

THE UNFORGIVING HEART HAS ...

Resistance—arguing about any advice or constructive criticism regarding the offender.

> "Do everything without complaining
> or arguing." (Philippians 2:14)

THE UNFORGIVING HEART IS ...

Impatient—exhibiting little patience while being easily provoked.

THE UNFORGIVING HEART HAS ...

Annoyance—feeling easily irritated by the offender.

> "A man's wisdom gives him patience;
> it is to his glory to overlook an offense."
> (Proverbs 19:11)

The Unforgiving Heart Is ...

Bitter—feeling weighed down with unresolved anger.

The Unforgiving Heart Has ...

Negativity—feeling no joy and no approval concerning the offender.

> "Each heart knows its own bitterness,
> and no one else can share its joy."
> (Proverbs 14:10)

Because of unforgiveness, the offended person becomes spiritually dry—trying to feel connected with God but lacking spiritual growth. As a direct result of unforgiveness, the offender's prayer life is blocked.

> "If you do not forgive men their sins,
> your Father will not forgive your sins."
> (Matthew 6:15)

QUESTION: "How can I forgive someone who has not apologized or shown any kind of repentance?"

ANSWER: Forgiveness has nothing to do with repentance. Forgiveness is not based on what the offender does or deserves, but rather on giving the gift of grace to your offender—a gift that is not deserved. The real question is: "Do you want to be Christlike?"

When Jesus was being crucified on the cross, His enemies had neither apologized nor repented, yet He extended His heart of forgiveness by praying,

*"Father, forgive them, for they
do not know what they are doing."
(Luke 23:34)*

QUESTION: "If I forgive those who offend me, I'll be a classic enabler. Why should offenders change if there is no consequence for their offensive behavior?"

ANSWER: Forgiveness is *not* enablement. If a man borrows money from you and later refuses to repay you, still you should forgive him. Release both him, as well as the offense, to God—for your sake, if for no other, so that you do not become bitter. But you should *not enter into another monetary relationship with him*. Do not give irresponsible people more opportunities to be irresponsible with you.

Enabling others means that by not establishing a boundary or by not having a consequence for when others violate a boundary, you *enable them to continue in their bad behavior*.

▶ Enablement puts you in a position of being offended again and again.

▶ Enabling never helps offenders change, but further ingrains their bad habits. However, one "consequence" to your offenders is that they will not have other opportunities to "use you" or offend you again.

▶ Enablers are classic people-pleasers who do not say *no* when they should say *no*. If you say *yes* to irresponsible people when you should say *no*, you are actually saying *no* to Christ. The apostle Paul said,

> "Am I now trying to win
> the approval of men, or of God?
> Or am I trying to please men?
> If I were still trying to please men,
> I would not be a servant of Christ."
> (Galatians 1:10)

When the Spirit of Christ is rooted within you, He produces fruit consistent with the character of Christ. The moment you entrust your life to Jesus, you are "sealed" with the Holy Spirit, who dwells within you for the rest of your life. (See Ephesians 1:13–14.) Just as orange trees produce oranges and banana trees produce bananas, the Spirit of Christ produces the character of Christ in a Christian. Therefore, the next time you are wronged, allow the Holy Spirit the freedom to produce His fruit of forgiveness in you.

> "The fruit of the Spirit is love, joy, peace, patience, kindness, goodness, faithfulness, gentleness and self-control."
> (Galatians 5:22–23)

THE FORGIVING HEART IS ...

Loving—not keeping a record of the bad things the offender has done.

THE FORGIVING HEART HAS ...

A *loving spirit*, allowing the possibility that the offender can change.

> "Above all, love each other deeply, because love covers over a multitude of sins."
> (1 Peter 4:8)

THE FORGIVING HEART IS ...

Joyous—taking to heart the goodness of God

and His sovereignty over all events in life, even the painful ones.

The Forgiving Heart Has ...

A *joyful awareness* that God will use trials to bring triumph.

"I will continue to rejoice, for I know that through ... the help given by the Spirit of Jesus Christ, what has happened to me will turn out for my deliverance."
(Philippians 1:18–19)

The Forgiving Heart Is ...

Peaceful—seeking to resolve any difficulty, hurt, or division and wanting the offender to be right with God and to be blessed by Him.

The Forgiving Heart Has ...

A *peaceful demeanor* that lowers the guard of the offender and paves the way for reconciliation.

"Peacemakers who sow in peace raise a harvest of righteousness."
(James 3:18)

The Forgiving Heart Is ...

Patient—accepting that the offender is not "fixed in cement" and could possibly change.

The Forgiving Heart Has ...

A *patient commitment* to wait for the right day to deal with difficulties and the right time to talk about them.

THE FORGIVING HEART IS ...

Kind—looking for and acting in practical ways to express kind deeds and to meet needs.

THE FORGIVING HEART HAS ...

A **kind deed** on behalf of the offender that is unexpected, unforeseen, and unannounced.

THE FORGIVING HEART IS ...

Good—holding to moral principles and purity even in the midst of controversy.

THE FORGIVING HEART HAS ...

A **good heart**, reflecting the highest moral character—the character of Christ.

THE FORGIVING HEART IS ...

Faithful—praying that those who have caused such pain might have changed lives.

THE FORGIVING HEART HAS ...

A **faithful commitment** to pray for those who have been hurtful.

The Forgiving Heart Is ...

Gentle—taking into account the woundedness of the offender and responding to harshness with a calm gentleness.

The Forgiving Heart Has ...

A *gentle response*, which understands that often "hurt people hurt people."

"A gentle answer turns away wrath,
but a harsh word stirs up anger."
(Proverbs 15:1)

The Forgiving Heart Is ...

Self-controlled—deciding ahead of time how to respond when conflict arises.

The Forgiving Heart Has ...

A *controlled response* that is Christlike so that, no matter what is said or done, there is a positive attitude toward the offender.

"Prepare your minds for action;
be self-controlled."
(1 Peter 1:13)

QUESTION: "How do I know whether I have genuinely forgiven someone?"

ANSWER: After someone has offended you, you can test the "quality" of your forgiveness by asking yourself the following questions:

▶ "Do I still expect my offender 'to pay' for the wrong done to me?"

▶ "Do I still have bitter feelings toward my offender?"

▶ "Do I still have vengeful thoughts toward my offender?"

To forgive someone does not in any way mean that you do not want justice, but it simply means that you are leaving the offense entirely in God's hands. You are refusing to harbor hateful feelings toward your offender. Remember, forgiveness is an ongoing process which requires that you choose to forgive every time the offense comes to mind, and that you choose to pray for the offender every time the offense crosses your mind.

"Far be it from me that I should sin against the Lord by failing to pray for you. And I will teach you the way that is good and right."
(1 Samuel 12:23)

Carrying around unforgiveness is like carrying a sack of cement all day long. If you hold unforgiveness in your heart, you are walking around with a weight that God never intended you to carry. Unforgiveness becomes a burden, and Jesus says, *"Come to me, all you who are weary and burdened, and I will give you rest"* (Matthew 11:28).

"Cast all your anxiety on him because he cares for you."
(1 Peter 5:7)

▶ *Unforgiveness* blocks the door to salvation and God's forgiveness.

▶ *Forgiveness* opens the door to salvation and God's forgiveness.

"If you forgive men when they sin against you, your heavenly Father will also forgive you. But if you do not forgive men their sins, your Father will not forgive your sins."
(Matthew 6:14–15)

▶ *Unforgiveness* allows a root of bitterness to grow.

▶ *Forgiveness* keeps a root of bitterness from growing.

"See to it that no one misses the grace of God and that no bitter root grows up to cause trouble and defile many."
(Hebrews 12:15)

▶ *Unforgiveness* opens a door to Satan in our lives.

▶ *Forgiveness* closes a door to Satan in our lives.

"I have forgiven in the sight of Christ for your sake, in order that Satan might not outwit us. For we are not unaware of his schemes." (2 Corinthians 2:10–11)

▶ *Unforgiveness* causes us to walk in darkness.

▶ *Forgiveness* brings us into the light.

"Anyone who claims to be in the light but hates his brother is still in the darkness. ... Whoever hates his brother is in the darkness and walks around in the darkness; he does not know where he is going, because the darkness has blinded him." (1 John 2:9–11)

▶ *Unforgiveness* is of Satan.

▶ *Forgiveness* is of God.

"If you harbor bitter envy and selfish ambition in your hearts . ... Such 'wisdom' does not come down from heaven but is earthly, unspiritual, of the devil." (James 3:14–15)

▶ *Unforgiveness* reflects a godless heart.

▶ *Forgiveness* reflects a godly heart.

> "The godless in heart
> harbor resentment."
> (Job 36:13)

▶ *Unforgiveness* makes us captive to sin.

▶ *Forgiveness* frees us.

> "I see that you are full of
> bitterness and captive to sin."
> (Acts 8:23)

▶ *Unforgiveness* grieves the Spirit of God.

▶ *Forgiveness* is empowered by the Spirit
of God.

> "Do not grieve the Holy Spirit of God,
> with whom you were sealed for the day
> of redemption. Get rid of all bitterness,
> rage and anger, brawling and slander,
> along with every form of malice."
> (Ephesians 4:30–31)

CAUSES OF UNFORGIVENESS

Amazingly, the Ten Boom's little home became the hub of the underground network. From their secret hiding place, the fingers of the underground reached into the farthest corners of Holland. As those of the Ten Boom family lived their double lives, they shuffled the hunted Jews into their one-room hiding place for sometimes up to two weeks, while members of the underground sought to slip the stowaways out of the country to safety.

Meanwhile, Corrie lived with the constant fear that they could be caught—and with reason. The family was betrayed by a fellow watchmaker whom Corrie's father had trained a few years earlier. As a result of this treachery, Corrie never embraced her father again nor delighted in the presence of her beloved sister Betsie.

How could Corrie not be consumed with bitterness toward this "friend" who betrayed them? She suffered the severity of these words:

> "Even my close friend, whom I trusted,
> he who shared my bread,
> has lifted up his heel against me."
> (Psalm 41:9)

People fail to forgive others for a variety of reasons. For example, when you have been deeply offended by a friend, forgiveness can make you feel emotionally "flat." In contrast, withholding forgiveness can make you feel emotionally pumped. Therefore, you may refuse to forgive the friend who offended you because of pride.[16] The Bible states it this way:

> "An offended brother is more
> unyielding than a fortified city."
> (Proverbs 18:19)

Barriers to Forgiveness[17]

▶ *No modeling of forgiveness from parents*

"I don't know how to forgive."

▶ *Denying that the offense ever occurred*

"I don't want to think about it."

▶ *Fearing to hold the guilty accountable*

"It's really all my fault." (This kind of thinking short-circuits the reality and the pain of being wronged.)

▶ *Not feeling that you can forgive yourself*

"No mercy for me—no mercy for you."

▶ *Not being forgiven for your past offenses*

"They didn't forgive me—why should I forgive them?"

▶ *Not understanding God's forgiveness*

"God will never forgive me—I will never forgive her."

▶ *Believing that bitterness is a required response to betrayal*

"God knows that my feelings are normal."

▶ *Thinking that forgiveness is excusing unjust behavior*

"I'm not about to say that what she did was okay!"

▶ *Requiring an apology or show of repentance*

"He shouldn't be forgiven because he's not really sorry."

▶ *Feeling a sense of power by hanging on to unforgiveness*

"He needs to see how wrong he is!"

▶ *Refusing to turn loose of revenge*

"He should pay for what he's done."

▶ *Harboring a prideful, hardened heart that becomes a spiritual stronghold*

"I refuse to forgive."

"Blessed is the man who always fears the
LORD, but he who hardens his heart
falls into trouble."
(Proverbs 28:14)

QUESTION: "What should I do if I don't want to reap the damaging results of unforgiveness?"

ANSWER: Choose to change your thinking and consciously ask God to soften your heart so that you will be willing to forgive. Unforgiveness can turn into an emotional stronghold that can damage many areas of your life. You do have control of what you dwell on. That is why the Bible says we are to …

"Take captive every thought to make it obedient to Christ."
(2 Corinthians 10:5)

We feel outraged when justice is denied. Thus, the cry for justice is common from everyone — everyone except the guilty person waiting to *receive* justice! Then the cry is not for justice, but for *mercy*.

> "Have mercy on me, O God, according to your unfailing love; according to your great compassion blot out my transgressions."
> (Psalm 51:1)

But why is the need for justice so strong and natural, and why is forgiveness so difficult and unnatural?

THREE REASONS:

#1 God has instilled within every human heart a *sense of right and wrong*; therefore, we feel a need for justice when we are wronged.

"The requirements of the law are written on their hearts [on the hearts of even the heathen]." (Romans 2:15)

#2 Based on the law, forgiveness seems *inappropriate and unnatural*.

"Show no pity: life for life, eye for eye, tooth for tooth, hand for hand, foot for foot." (Deuteronomy 19:21)

#3 Because God is a God of justice, *somebody has to pay*. That Somebody was Jesus. The death of Jesus on the cross fulfilled the justice of God. (See Romans 3:25–26.) In the same way that God needed to have His justice satisfied by Jesus' dying on the cross, shouldn't we expect justice before we extend mercy and forgiveness?

The truth is that although everyone must face *God's justice*, Jesus was the payment for *everyone's* wrongs. While governments execute justice, *individually* we are to extend mercy. We are to leave *individual* justice to God. The Bible exhorts us to …

"Be merciful, just as your Father is merciful." (Luke 6:36)

In a military war, if your enemy gains a "foothold," that means your enemy has gained some of your ground. Your enemy has taken some of your territory. Now, with that foothold, your foe has a secure base from which there can be further advance.

If you have been hurt and as a result harbor anger in your heart, realize that your *unresolved anger* can be a foothold for the enemy. The Bible says,

> "'In your anger do not sin':
> Do not let the sun go down while you are
> still angry, and do not give the devil a
> foothold." (Ephesians 4:26–27)

The Development of a Spiritual Stronghold

1. When you refuse to forgive your offender, you have *unresolved anger.*

2. Unresolved anger, in turn, allows Satan to set up a *stronghold in your mind.*

3. This stronghold is a *fortified place* from which *"flaming arrows of the evil one"* are flung (Ephesians 6:16).

4. These flaming arrows of accusation and unforgiveness can continue to burn in your heart and keep you *mentally captive to do the enemy's will.*

At this point you are engaged in spiritual warfare. In order to win the spiritual war, recognize that the battle for freedom is fought in your mind. You need to take captive every thought of unforgiveness and release your unresolved anger to God.

"You must rid yourselves of all such things as these: anger, rage, malice, slander, and filthy language from your lips."
(Colossians 3:8)

Spiritual Warfare Prayer

The following spiritual warfare prayer will help you to honestly confront and release your anger to God and thereby rid yourself of such damaging habits.

"Dear Heavenly Father,

▶ I don't want to be defeated in my life. Thank You that Jesus, who lives in me, is greater than Satan, who is in the world. (Read 1 John 4:4.)

▶ I know I have been bought with the price of Christ's blood, which was shed at Calvary. My body is not my own—it belongs to Christ. (Read 1 Corinthians 6:19–20.)

▶ Right now, I refuse all thoughts that are not from You. (Read 2 Corinthians 10:3–5.)

▶ I choose to forgive those who have hurt me, and I choose to release all of my pain and anger into Your hands. (Read Colossians 3:13.)

▶ I resist Satan and all his power. (Read James 4:7.)

▶ As I stand in the full armor of God, I ask You to bind Satan and his demonic forces from having any influence over me. (Read Ephesians 6:11.)

▶ From now on, with the shield of faith, I will deflect and defeat every unforgiving thought that could defeat me. (Read Ephesians 6:16.)

▶ And I yield my life to Your plan and Your purpose. (Read Jeremiah 29:11.)

In the holy name of Jesus I pray. Amen."

You can't truly forgive others until you have God's forgiveness in your own life. Of all the world's religions, only the Bible teaches that God forgives sin completely.[18] God is ready to forgive each and every one of our offenses. Yet, many refuse His forgiveness because they don't understand mercy and grace.

▶ Grace is getting what you don't deserve (forgiveness and heaven).

▶ Mercy is not getting what you do deserve (unforgiveness and hell).

Right now, God wants to show you His mercy and grace. Through Jesus Christ, God wants to give you His forgiveness—forgiveness that is found only in a secure relationship with Him.

How Can You Find God's Forgiveness?

#1 God's Purpose for You is *Salvation.*

What was God's motive in sending Christ to earth? To condemn you?

No … to express His love for you by saving you!

"God so loved the world that he gave his one and only Son, that whoever believes in him shall not perish but have eternal life. For God

did not send his Son into the world to condemn the world, but to save the world through him." (John 3:16–17)

What was Jesus' purpose in coming to earth? To make everything perfect and to remove all sin?

No ... to forgive your sins, empower you to have victory over sin, and enable you to live a fulfilled life!

"I [Jesus] have come that they may have life, and have it to the full." (John 10:10)

#2 Your Problem is *Sin*.

What exactly is sin?

Sin is living *independently* of God's standard— knowing what is right, but choosing wrong.

"Anyone, then, who knows the good he ought to do and doesn't do it, sins." (James 4:17)

What is the major consequence of sin?

Spiritual death, spiritual separation from God.

"The wages of sin is death, but the gift of God is eternal life in Christ Jesus our Lord." (Romans 6:23)

#3 God's Provision for You is the *Savior*.

Can anything remove the penalty for sin?

Yes. Jesus died on the cross to personally pay the penalty for your sins.

"God demonstrates his own love for us in this: While we were still sinners, Christ died for us." (Romans 5:8)

What is the solution to being separated from God?

Belief in Jesus Christ as the only way to God the Father.

"Jesus answered, 'I am the way and the truth and the life. No one comes to the Father except through me.'" (John 14:6)

#4 Your Part is *Surrender.*

Place your faith in (rely on) Jesus Christ as your personal Lord and Savior and reject your "good works" as a means of gaining God's approval.

"It is by grace you have been saved, through faith—and this not from yourselves, it is the gift of God—not by works, so that no one can boast." (Ephesians 2:8–9)

Give Christ control of your life, entrusting yourself to Him.

"Jesus said to his disciples, 'If anyone would come after me, he must deny himself and take up his cross and follow me. For whoever wants to save his life will lose it, but whoever loses his life for me will find it. What good will it be for a man if he gains the whole world, yet forfeits his soul?'" (Matthew 16:24–26)

The moment you choose to believe in Him—entrusting your life to Christ—He gives you His Spirit to live inside you. Then the Spirit of Christ enables you to live the fulfilled life God has planned for you, and He gives you His power to forgive others so that your heart can begin to heal.

If you want to be fully forgiven by God and become the person God created you to be, you can tell Him in a simple, heartfelt prayer like this:

PRAYER OF SALVATION

*"God, I want a real relationship with You.
I admit that many times I've chosen to go
my own way instead of Your way.
Please forgive me for my sins.
Jesus, thank You for dying on the cross
to pay the penalty for my sins.
Come into my life to be my Lord
and my Savior.
Give me Your power to practice forgiveness
and to love those who have wounded me.
Begin healing the hurts in my life
with Your love and make me the person
You created me to be.
In Your holy name I pray. Amen."*

What Can You Expect Now?

If you sincerely prayed this prayer, look at what God says!

"In him [Jesus] we have redemption through his blood, the forgiveness of sins, in accordance with the riches of God's grace that he lavished on us with all wisdom and understanding."
(Ephesians 1:7–8)

QUESTION: "I know God has forgiven me of my sins, but how do I forgive myself?"

ANSWER: Have you ever considered that being unwilling to forgive what God has forgiven is discrediting God's gift of mercy toward you? It is placing yourself as a higher judge than God Himself. It is saying:

▶ "God, you are wrong in forgiving me because I don't deserve to be forgiven."

▶ "Christ's sacrifice on the cross must not be sufficient to cleanse me of my sins."

▶ "Something else must be done to make up for what is lacking in Jesus' sacrifice."

While not forgiving yourself may make you *feel* like you are being *humble before God*, realize that in such a situation your focus is not on God but on yourself. Humility is bowing your knee to God and submitting to His authority and His right to declare righteous whomever He chooses. After all, who are you to overrule God? Since

Satan is an "accuser" of Christians (Revelation 12:10), when you continue blaming yourself, you align yourself with Satan, whose goal is to keep you feeling defeated. Instead, humbly thank God for His undeserved mercy. Thank Him for His undeserved grace and live in His undeserved forgiveness.

"He saved us, not because of righteous things we had done, but because of his mercy. He saved us through the washing of rebirth and renewal by the Holy Spirit."
(Titus 3:5)

Everyone has been created with three God-given needs—the needs for love, for significance, and for security.[19] Many people who have been hurt feel insignificant and powerless; therefore, they try to get their need for significance met by withholding forgiveness. Unforgiveness gives them a sense of power and superiority.

If you were ever betrayed by a friend, for a time you may have felt powerless to stop the pain. Since no one likes to feel powerless, unforgiveness provides an illusion of power. By refusing to forgive, you feel a sense of power. By holding on to hatred, you feel infused with strength. By retaliating with revenge, you carry out a power play.

▶ **WRONG BELIEF:** "It's natural for me to resent those who have wronged me. If I forgive them, they will get away with it. My offenders need to pay for the wrongs committed against me."

RESULT: This belief reflects an attitude of pride that sets you up as a judge higher than God Himself—God, who is willing to forgive and forget.

"I, even I, am he who blots out your transgressions, for my own sake, and remembers your sins no more."
(Isaiah 43:25)

▶**RIGHT BELIEF:** "Because God has totally forgiven me, I can release my resentment and choose to forgive others. I will rely on Christ, who is living within me, to forgive through me."

RESULT: This belief reflects a heart of humility that results in a desire to forgive others in the same way God forgives you.

"If you forgive men when they sin against you, your heavenly Father will also forgive you. But if you do not forgive men their sins, your Father will not forgive your sins."
(Matthew 6:14–15)

STEPS TO SOLUTION

After she had survived the suffering of concentration camps (living in flea and rat infested barracks, losing her father and sister to inhumane treatment, facing death on a daily basis herself, and coping with what seemed to be the triumph of evil), life for Corrie should be basically easy—or one would assume. Wouldn't future problems pale in comparison to the horrors of her past? But by Corrie's own admission, she could not sleep at night—at least not until she made the determined decision to *choose* forgiveness on a daily basis and then to act on that decision each day. Corrie's admission is amazingly honest.

> I wish I could say that after a long and fruitful life, traveling the world, I had learned to forgive all my enemies. I wish I could say that merciful and charitable thoughts just naturally flowed from me and on to others. But they don't. If there is one thing I have learned … it's that I can't store up good feelings and behavior—but only draw them fresh from God each day.[20]

Corrie ten Boom learned that she not only needed to be forgiven by God, but also that she needed to forgive as God forgives. She needed to show mercy, for Jesus said ...

"Go and learn what this means: 'I desire mercy, not sacrifice.' For I have not come to call the righteous, but sinners."
(Matthew 9:13)

The obvious answer to the question, "Why forgive?" is this: "Because God says so!" But *why does God say so*? First, because *others* need it. And second, because we need it![21] Long ago, George Herbert said that the person who cannot forgive "breaks the bridge over which all must pass if they would ever reach heaven; for everyone has need to be forgiven."[22]

God's Heart on Forgiveness

▶ *God commands* that we forgive each other.

"Be kind and compassionate to one another, forgiving each other, just as in Christ God forgave you." (Ephesians 4:32)

▶ *God wants* us to forgive others because He forgives us.

"Bear with each other and forgive whatever grievances you may have against one another. Forgive as the Lord forgave you." (Colossians 3:13)

▶ *God wants* us to see unforgiveness as sin.

"Anyone, then, who knows the good he ought to do and doesn't do it, sins." (James 4:17)

▶ *God wants* us to get rid of unforgiveness and have a heart of mercy.

"Blessed are the merciful, for they will be shown mercy." (Matthew 5:7)

▶ *God wants* us to do our part to live in peace with everyone.

"If it is possible, as far as it depends on you, live at peace with everyone." (Romans 12:18)

▶ *God wants* us to overcome evil with good.

"Do not be overcome by evil, but overcome evil with good." (Romans 12:21)

▶ *God wants* us to be ministers of reconciliation.

"God ... reconciled us to himself through Christ and gave us the ministry of reconciliation: that God was reconciling the world to himself in Christ, not counting men's sins against them. And he has committed to us the message of reconciliation." (2 Corinthians 5:18–19)

The Parable of
the Unmerciful Servant
Matthew 18:23–35

Jesus told a parable about a servant who owed the king ten thousand talents (about $50,000,000 today). The king ordered that the servant and his family be sold—literally—along with all that they had. The servant fell on his knees begging for mercy, "I will pay back everything." The king extended mercy and forgave the entire debt.

The king represents our heavenly Father, who *forgives all of our debt* of sin when we sincerely come to Him for forgiveness and mercy. (vv. 23–27)

Later this same servant grabbed one of his fellow servants who owed him a hundred denarii (about $50 today) and demanded repayment. His fellow servant fell to his knees begging for mercy, "I will pay you back." Instead, the first servant had the man thrown into prison until he could pay the debt.

The servant who had his debts removed was *not willing to forgive* the debts of another servant who sought forgiveness. (vv. 28–30)

When the other servants saw what had happened, they were greatly distressed and told the king about it. The cruel servant was called by the king, who was angered that his servant had not extended the mercy he himself had received from the king. The servant was then thrown into jail to be tortured until he could pay all he owed.

If we don't extend *true forgiveness to others*, our Father in heaven will not forgive us. (vv. 31–35)

> "This is how my heavenly Father will treat each of you unless you forgive your brother from your heart." (Matthew 18:35)

Key Verse to Memorize

Have you ever prayed "the model prayer" or what is often called "The Lord's Prayer"? If so, did you mean it? Think about it—did you *really* mean it?

Jesus said, "Forgive us our debts, as we also have forgiven our debtors" (Matthew 6:12).

If you really meant these words, then you are asking God to forgive you in *the same exact way* you have forgiven those who have wronged you. That is why the Bible says,

> "Bear with each other and forgive whatever grievances you may have against one another. Forgive as the Lord forgave you." (Colossians 3:13)

Have you ever noticed that the word *forgiveness* has the little word "give" in it? When you choose to forgive, you *give* someone a *gift*—the gift of freedom from having to pay the penalty for offending you, and the gift of dismissing the debt owed to you!

Because this can be a difficult "gift" to give, you may need to travel through four stages of forgiveness. But realize that you are also giving yourself a gift ... the gift of "grudge-free living." That is true freedom. And that is why the Bible says, *"Do not seek revenge or bear a grudge against one of your people, but love your neighbor as yourself."* (Leviticus 19:18)

1 FACE THE OFFENSE.

When you feel pain that is *personal*, *unfair*, and *deep*, you have a wound that can be healed only by forgiving the one who wounded you. First you must face the truth of what has actually been done and not hinder true healing by rationalizing and focusing on false thinking.

▶ *Don't minimize the offense by thinking*: "No matter how badly he treats me, it's okay."

TRUTH: Bad treatment is not okay. There is no excuse for bad treatment of any kind—any time.

"Have nothing to do with the fruitless

deeds of darkness, but rather expose them."
(Ephesians 5:11)

▶ **Don't excuse the offender's behavior by thinking**: "He doesn't mean to hurt me. I shouldn't feel upset with him—he's a member of my family!"

TRUTH: No matter the age of the offender or our relationship, we need to call sin "sin." We need to face the truth instead of trying to change it. There must first be a guilty party in order to have someone to forgive.

"Whoever says to the guilty, 'You are innocent'— peoples will curse him." (Proverbs 24:24)

▶ **Don't assume that quick forgiveness is full forgiveness by thinking**:[23] "As soon as that horrendous ordeal occurred, I quickly and fully forgave him. That's what I've been taught to do!"

TRUTH: Many well-intentioned people feel guilty if they don't extend immediate forgiveness so they "forgive" quickly. Yet they have neither faced the full impact of the offense nor grieved over what actually happened. Rarely is the full impact of sin felt at the moment it occurs. Rather, its impact is felt at different levels over a period of time. Therefore, forgiveness needs to be extended at each of these levels. "Quick forgiveness" over deep hurts may seem sufficient, but it is not "full forgiveness"— not until it has been extended at each level of impact. Before complete forgiveness can be extended, you must face the truth about the gravity of the offense and its extended impact on you.

"You [God] desire truth in the inner parts; you teach me wisdom in the inmost place." (Psalm 51:6)

2 FEEL THE OFFENSE.[24]

We usually do not hate strangers or acquaintances; we just "get angry" with strangers. But Lewis Smedes writes, "When a person destroys what our commitment and our intimacy created, something precious is destroyed."[25] Then anger or even hatred may be our true feeling in response to deep, unfair pain. Hatred toward an offender needs to be brought up out of the basement of our souls and dealt with. However, not all hatred is wrong. God *hates* evil.

"There is a time for everything, and a season for every activity under heaven ... a time to love and a time to hate." (Ecclesiastes 3:1, 8)

Failing to feel the offense results in ...

▶ **Denying your pain:** "I don't blame her for always criticizing me. She is under a lot of pressure, and it doesn't hurt me."

TRUTH: Being mistreated by someone you love is painful. Feeling the pain must take place before healing can take place.

"The LORD is close to the broken hearted and saves those who are crushed in spirit." (Psalm 34:18)

▶ **Carrying false guilt:** "I feel guilty if I hate what was done to me. I'm never supposed to have hatred."

TRUTH: God hates sin. You too can hate sin. You are to hate the sin, but not the sinner.

"To fear the LORD is to hate evil; I hate pride and arrogance, evil behavior and perverse speech." (Proverbs 8:13)

3 FORGIVE THE OFFENDER.

We are called by God to forgive! And when you do forgive, genuine forgiveness draws you into the heart of God, and your life takes on the divine character of Christ.

▶ **ARGUMENT:** "I don't think it is right to forgive when I don't feel like forgiving."

ANSWER: Forgiveness is not a feeling, but is rather an act of the will—a choice. Jesus established what was right when He said,

"When you stand praying, if you hold anything against anyone, forgive him, so that your Father in heaven may forgive you your sins." (Mark 11:25)

▶ **ARGUMENT:** "I can forgive everyone else, but I don't have the power to forgive that person."

ANSWER: The issue is not your lack of power to forgive, but rather how strong God's power is within you to forgive any sin committed against you.

"His divine power has given us everything we need for life and godliness through our knowledge of him who called us by his own glory and goodness." (2 Peter 1:3)

▶ **ARGUMENT:** "Forgiveness isn't fair. She ought to pay for her wrong!"

ANSWER: God knows how to deal with each person fairly—and He will, in His own time.

"Do not take revenge, my friends, but leave room for God's wrath, for it is written: 'It is mine to avenge; I will repay,' says the Lord." (Romans 12:19)

▶ **ARGUMENT:** "I can't keep forgiving—he keeps doing the same thing over and over."

ANSWER: You cannot control what others do, but you can control how you respond to what others do. Jesus said you are to respond with forgiveness no matter the number of times wronged. The apostle Peter asked Jesus,

"'Lord, how many times shall I forgive my brother when he sins against me? Up to seven times?' Jesus answered, 'I tell you, not seven times, but seventy-seven times.'" (Matthew 18:21–22)

▶ **ARGUMENT:** "I cannot forgive and forget. I keep thinking about being hurt."[26]

ANSWER: When you choose to forgive, you don't get a case of "holy amnesia." However, after facing the hurt and confronting the offender, close off your mind to rehearsing the pain of the past. Forget about your pain. Refuse to focus on your hurt.

"Brothers, I do not consider myself yet to have taken hold of it. But one thing I do: Forgetting what is behind and straining toward what is ahead, I press on toward the goal to win the prize for which God has called me heavenward in Christ Jesus." (Philippians 3:13–14)

4 FIND ONENESS IF APPROPRIATE.

Relationships filled with resentment ultimately perish—relationships filled with forgiveness ultimately prevail. However, reconciliation in a relationship—the restoration of oneness— is contingent on several vital factors. When these conditions are met, when both parties are committed to *honesty in the relationship*, there is real hope that the two can be of one mind and one heart again.[27] The Bible says,

"If you have any encouragement from being united with Christ, if any comfort from his love, if any fellowship with the Spirit, if any tenderness and compassion, then make my joy complete by being like-minded, having the same love, being one in spirit and purpose." (Philippians 2:1–2)

Honesty Required for Reconciliation

H—HONESTLY evaluate yourself and your relationship.

God intends to use your relationships to reveal your weaknesses and to strengthen your relationship with Him. The first step toward reconciliation is to honestly evaluate your own weaknesses and the weaknesses within your relationships so that you can know where change needs to take place.

"Search me, O God, and know my heart; test me and know my anxious thoughts. See if there is any offensive way in me, and lead me in the way everlasting." (Psalm 139:23–24)

O—OPEN your heart and share your pain.

Have a candid conversation with your offender. Fully explain the pain you have suffered and the sorrow in your heart. Don't attack your offender. Instead, address the offense and share how it made you feel.

"If your brother sins against you, go and show him his fault, just between the two of you. If he listens to you, you have won your brother over." (Matthew 18:15)

N—NOTICE whether your offender takes responsibility.

Offenders need to know that what they did struck like an arrow into your heart. They need to *feel* your hurt. If offenders ignore your pain and respond with how much you have hurt them, they are not ready for reconciliation because they are not ready to take responsibility. They need to care about your pain as much as they care about their own pain. They need to indicate a godly sorrow.

"Godly sorrow brings repentance that leads to salvation and leaves no regret, but worldly sorrow brings death." (2 Corinthians 7:10)

E—EXPECT your offender to be completely truthful.

Promises need to be made regarding honesty, support, and loyalty within the relationship. Although you cannot guarantee someone else's dependability, you should be able to discern whether there is sincerity and truthfulness.

"Truthful lips endure forever, but a lying tongue lasts only a moment." (Proverbs 12:19)

S—SET appropriate boundaries for the relationship.

You may have a heart for reconciliation; however, you need to evaluate, *Has my offender crossed the line regarding what is appropriate (excessively angry, possessive, demeaning, insensitive, irresponsible, prideful, abusive)?* If so, explain what the boundary line is, what the repercussion is for crossing the boundary (a limited relationship), and what the reward is for staying within the boundary (increased trust). You need to be disciplined enough to hold your offender accountable, and your offender needs to become disciplined enough to stop hurting the relationship.

"He who heeds discipline shows the way to life, but whoever ignores correction leads others astray." (Proverbs 10:17)

T—TAKE time, cautiously think, and sincerely pray before you let your offender all the way back into your heart.

When trust has been trampled, time, integrity, and consistency are needed to prove that your offender is now trustworthy. Change takes time. Therefore, don't rush the relationship. Confidence is not regained overnight. Trust is not given, but earned.

"Above all else, guard your heart, for it is the wellspring of life." (Proverbs 4:23)

Y—YIELD your heart to starting over.

God wants you to have a heart that is yielded to His perfect will for your life. Serious offenses will reshape your future, and you will not be able to come back together with your offender as though nothing ever happened. You personally change through pain. You take on new roles, and you cannot simply abandon your new places in life the moment a friend is forgiven and is invited back into your heart and life. Leave negative patterns in the past and establish positive patterns of relating.

"Forget the former things; do not dwell on the past. See, I am doing a new thing! Now it springs up; do you not perceive it? I am making a way in the desert and streams in the wasteland." (Isaiah 43:18–19)

QUESTION: "If I have forgiven a monetary debt, thus freeing a person from paying me back, does God still expect that person to repay the debt as a matter of integrity?"

ANSWER: You should not expect anything back *if you have truly forgiven the debt*. However, God expects us to be people of integrity—people who keep our word, honor our agreements, and fulfill our obligations. We should do everything within our power to *avoid* acquiring debts that we cannot pay and to repay all debts that we now owe. If you have forgiven a debt that a person is *now able to repay*, then that person should offer to repay the debt as a matter of integrity. But you are not to expect that. Consider two situations:

▶ **Debtor #1**

A friend borrows $100 from you and promises to pay you back in one month. But because of an accident, he becomes disabled and loses his job. He has no way of repaying the debt. If six weeks later you forgive your friend's debt, does the person still owe the debt?

No, *the issue of repayment is not a matter of integrity before God, but is simply a matter of inability*—an inability to repay the debt. God knows that there are times when circumstances make the payment of a debt impossible. If later your friend has the ability to repay some amount, whether it is $1.00 or $10.00 a week, he could come to you and *make the offer* to repay as he can. If you state again that you want him not to feel compelled to repay you, then with deepest gratitude, he should accept your generosity as a gift of grace.

▶ **Debtor #2**

A friend borrows $100 from you and promises to pay you back in one month, yet makes no effort to repay the money. After six months, you forgive the debt. Does he still owe the debt?

No, *repayment of the debt is not owed to you* because you have forgiven it. However, a person of integrity will want to repay the debt. Whether he begins paying back $1.00 or $10.00 a week, *the repayment is owed as a matter of integrity before God*.

Interestingly, according to the Law, the Israelites were *required* to cancel debts *at the end of every seventh year*. If we hold on to extended expectation of repayment and the debt is not repaid, we would likely become bitter; such bitterness is detrimental to all involved. (Read Hebrews 12:15.)

"At the end of every seven years
you must cancel debts. ...
Every creditor shall cancel the loan he has
made to his fellow Israelite. He shall not
require payment from his fellow Israelite or
brother, because the Lᴏʀᴅ's time for
canceling debts has been proclaimed."
(Deuteronomy 15:1–2)

PRAYER TO FORGIVE YOUR OFFENDER

*"Lord Jesus, thank You for caring about
how much my heart has been hurt.
You know the pain I have felt
because of* (list every offense).
*Right now I release all that
pain into Your hands.
Thank You, Lord, for dying on the cross for
me and extending Your forgiveness to me.
As an act of my will,
I choose to forgive* (name).
Right now, I move (name) *off of
my emotional hook to Your hook.
I refuse all thoughts of revenge.
I trust that in Your time and in Your way
You will deal with* (name) *as You see fit.
And Lord, thank You for giving me Your
power to forgive so that I can be set free.
In Your precious name I pray. Amen."*

Have you ever said, "I was severely wronged by someone I once trusted. People want me to forgive, but how can I simply let my offender off the hook?" If these words have passed your lips or even rolled around in your mind, be assured that you are not alone. That is precisely why you need to know how to handle "the hook."

How to Handle "The Hook"

▶ Make a list of all the offenses caused by your offender.

▶ Imagine right now that a hook is attached to your collarbone. Then imagine all the pain attached to the hook as a result of the wrong that was done to you.

▶ Ask yourself, *Do I really want to carry all that pain with me for the rest of my life?* The Lord wants you to take the pain from the past and release it into His hands.

▶ Then take the one who offended you off your emotional hook and place your offender onto God's hook. The Lord knows how to deal with your offender in His time and in His way. God says ...

> "It is mine to avenge; I will repay."
> (Deuteronomy 32:35)

In the Olympics, a boxer doesn't simply step into the ring and register a knockout with the first punch. Most often, it takes many rounds of exchanging many blows before a winner is announced. For the most part, forgiveness is not a onetime event.[28] We may need to go through many bouts of forgiving as a part of the *process of forgiveness*. But if we confront our hurts and face our wounds, it will be worth the emotional bruises we will likely encounter. As we consistently release each recurring thought of an offense, eventually the thoughts will stay away. The process will be complete. The fight will be won. Jesus emphasized the "again and again" nature of forgiveness when He said ...

"If he [your brother] sins against you seven times in a day, and seven times comes back to you and says, 'I repent,' forgive him."
(Luke 17:4)

How to Forgive ... Again

F—FORBID recurring thoughts of the wrongs done to enter your mind. Stop them as soon as they occur. Boldly say to yourself, "I refuse to keep a record of this. I refuse to keep a ledger."

"[Love] keeps no record of wrongs."
(1 Corinthians 13:5)

O—OVERCOME the temptation to bring up the matter again. After an honest confrontation with the offender and both sides of the situation have been dealt with—or if the other person refuses to talk about the problem—let the Holy Spirit do His work of conviction. Ecclesiastes 3:7 says, "*[There is] a time to be silent and a time to speak.*" Pray this passage:

"Set a guard over my mouth, O LORD; keep watch over the door of my lips." (Psalm 141:3)

R—REPEAT SCRIPTURE in your mind. Allow God's perspective to change your perspective. Allow God's heart to permeate your heart. At times of testing, repeat over and over, "Love covers this wrong. Lord, may I be an expression of Your love. May I reflect Your love that covers over all wrongs."

"Hatred stirs up dissension, but love covers over all wrongs." (Proverbs 10:12)

G—GIVE the situation to God. Jesus understands how much you have been wronged. When He was being persecuted, Jesus knew that the heavenly Father would judge justly … in His way, in His time. And you can know the same. Your trial will make you either bitter or better. Say to the Lord, "I put my heart into Your hands. I entrust myself to You. I know You will judge this situation justly." These words were said about Jesus:

"When they hurled their insults at him, he did not retaliate; when he suffered, he made no threats. Instead, he entrusted himself to him who judges justly." (1 Peter 2:23)

I—INTERCEDE on behalf of your offender. God does not present prayer as an option for you; it is a command. When you have been wronged, pray, "LORD, give me eyes to see him through Your eyes. May I care for her with Your care."

"Far be it from me that I should sin against the Lord by failing to pray for you." (1 Samuel 12:23)

V—VALUE what you can give rather than what you can receive. Pray for God to help you understand the offender's past and how his or her inner pain has contributed to the injury you are now experiencing. Focus on how you might meet some of these inner needs, for it is more blessed to give than to receive.

"The Lord Jesus himself said: 'It is more blessed to give than to receive.'" (Acts 20:35)

E—EXTEND God's grace, mercy, and forgiveness. Forgiveness is a direct expression of both God's grace and God's mercy. Grace is getting what you don't deserve (pardon). Mercy is not getting what you do deserve (punishment). Pray often, "Lord, may my life be an expression of Your grace and an extension of Your mercy."

"The Lord is full of compassion and mercy." (James 5:11)

Jesus said, *"Love your enemies."* Impossible! Unrealistic! No way! People *can't* love their enemies! At least that's the assumption. Yet the Greek word *agape*, translated "love" in this passage, by definition means "a commitment to seek the highest good of another person."[29] The "highest good" for those who are genuinely *wrong* is that their hearts become genuinely *right*. What can be one major catalyst for this change? Jesus provides the answer:

> "Love your enemies and pray for those who persecute you." (Matthew 5:44)

If you are saying, "But they really aren't enemies," realize that if someone evokes resentment, bitterness, or hatred, that person is an enemy to your spirit. Because praying for your enemy is commanded by Christ, believers should obey this directive and not regard this kind of prayer as optional. And because praying for your enemy protects your heart from bitterness, you should *want* to obey this directive in heart and in deed. One approach is to pray "the fruit of the Spirit" for your offender. And because you are willing to "bless" your enemy, the Bible says that you will inherit a blessing.

> "Do not repay evil with evil or insult with insult, but with blessing, because to this you were called so that you may inherit a blessing." (1 Peter 3:9)

How to Pray for Those Who Hurt You

"The fruit of the Spirit is love, joy,
peace, patience, kindness, goodness,
faithfulness, gentleness and self-control.
Against such things there is no law."
(Galatians 5:22–23)

▶ "*Lord*, I pray that (*name*) will be filled with *the fruit of love* by becoming fully aware of Your unconditional *love*—and in turn will be able to *love* others.

▶ "*Lord*, I pray that (*name*) will be filled with *the fruit of joy* because of experiencing Your steady *joy*—and in turn will radiate that inner *joy* to others.

▶ "*Lord*, I pray that (*name*) will be filled with *the fruit of peace*—Your inner *peace*—and in turn will have a *peace* that passes all understanding toward others.

▶ "*Lord*, I pray that (*name*) will be filled with *the fruit of patience* because of experiencing Your *patience*—and in turn will extend that same extraordinary *patience* to others.

▶ "*Lord*, I pray that (*name*) will be filled with *the fruit of kindness* because of experiencing Your *kindness*—and in turn will extend that same undeserved *kindness* to others.

▶ "*Lord*, I pray that (*name*) will be filled with *the fruit of goodness* because of experiencing the genuine *goodness* of Jesus—and in turn will reflect the moral *goodness* of Jesus before others.

▶ "***Lord***, I pray that (*name*) will be filled with ***the fruit of faithfulness*** because of realizing Your amazing *faithfulness*—and in turn will desire to be *faithful* to You, to Your Word, and to others.

▶ "***Lord***, I pray that (*name*) will be filled with ***the fruit of gentleness*** because of experiencing Your *gentleness*—and in turn will be able to be *gentle* with others.

▶ "***Lord***, I pray that (*name*) will be filled with ***the fruit of self-control***—the *control by Christ of self*—and in turn will rely on His *control* for enablement to break out of bondage and to be an example before others.

In the name of Jesus I pray. Amen."

"The wisdom that comes from heaven
is first of all pure; then peace-loving,
considerate, submissive, full of mercy and
good fruit, impartial and sincere."
(James 3:17)

QUESTION: "How can I release the bitterness toward my offender, who is now dead?"

ANSWER: Although you cannot confront your offender in person, you can confront indirectly by saying what you would want to say or need to say as though your offender is in front of you.

Consider the "chair technique." Imagine the

person seated in a chair placed in front of you. Say the things you would say to the person if you were actually seated across a table from one another. Express your feelings about what was done to you and the painful ramifications those events have had on your life. Then forgive the person and explain that you have taken the person off of your emotional hook and placed the person onto God's hook.

▶ Write a letter to your offender, stating every painful memory. Read it over the person's grave or at a place where you can openly speak to the person as though you were in each other's presence. Then at the close, choose to forgive by releasing your offender into the hands of God.

▶ Make a list of all painful as well as positive memories. After completing the list, go back to the beginning and write the word "past" by each memory. Acknowledge and accept that the past is in the past. Release all the pain as well as the person into the hands of God.

▶ The fact that your offender has died does not mean that you cannot forgive and thereby prevent bitterness from establishing a foothold in your heart and mind. The Bible says,

"See to it that no one misses the grace of God and that no bitter root grows up to cause trouble and defile many."
(Hebrews 12:15)

Playing the Blame Game

Often the way people justify acting badly toward others is by focusing on the guilt of others. Your offenders will want to blame you for *your guilt* so as to relieve *their own guilt*. Even if they are 98% wrong, by blaming you for your 2%, they feel justified, and their scale of justification is balanced. This means they will not feel the full weight (conviction) for their sin.

Offender feels justified

Your offenders may be able to balance the scale with your guilt, but they still haven't emptied the scale of their guilt. And every time they begin to feel guilty for whatever wrong *they have done*, they must blame you for what *you have done*.

Therefore, they stay in bondage to keeping the scales balanced. Realize, however, that even if you are not the major guilty party, you are still responsible before God for your percentage of wrong—even if it is only 2%!

> "If we claim to be without sin, we deceive ourselves and the truth is not in us."
> (1 John 1:8)

Ending the Blame Game

Regardless of how much someone else has been wrong, you are responsible to ask forgiveness for your own area of wrong. Jesus said ...

> "If you are offering your gift at the altar
> and there remember that your brother
> has something against you,
> leave your gift there in front of the altar.
> First go and be reconciled to your brother;
> then come and offer your gift"
> (Matthew 5:23–24).

▶ When you humbly ask forgiveness for your sin, your guilt is removed and the blame game is over.

▶ When your blame is lifted off the scale, the weight of your offender's guilt comes down heavily! This is why, when one person asks, "Will you forgive me?" often the other person responds with, "Yes, but will you also forgive me?"

▶ When you have a spirit of humility, the Spirit of God can use your humble heart to bring godly conviction to your offender's heart.

True freedom can be found only by keeping the scale of justification empty by asking forgiveness from those you have wronged and extending forgiveness to those who have wronged you.

"I strive always to keep my conscience clear before God and man." (Acts 24:16)

Blame is lifted when sin is forgiven

True freedom is found when scales are empty

The horrors of World War II are now far behind Corrie, but the horrors of the war between forgiveness and unforgiveness still rage. How can she find the strength to take the hand of someone who represents the evil regime that destroyed the two people she held most dear? How can she forgive this man? To Corrie's dismay, she discovers she cannot!

His hand was thrust out to shake mine. And I, who had preached so often ... the need to forgive, kept my hand at my side.

Even as the angry, vengeful thoughts boiled through me, I saw the sin of them. Jesus Christ had died for this man; was I going to ask for more? Lord Jesus, I prayed, forgive me and help me to forgive him.

I tried to smile. I struggled to raise my hand. I could not. I felt nothing, not the slightest spark of warmth or charity. And so again I breathed a silent prayer. Jesus, I cannot forgive him. Give me Your forgiveness.

As I took his hand, the most incredible thing happened. From my shoulder along my arm and through my hand a current seemed to pass from me to him, while into my heart sprang a love for this stranger that almost overwhelmed me.

And so I discovered that it is not on our forgiveness any more than on our goodness that the world's healing hinges, but on His. When He tells us to love our enemies, He gives, along with the command, the love itself.[31]

Jesus would never tell you to *"love your enemies, do good to those who hate you"* (Luke 6:27) without giving you the power to do it. And Corrie ten Boom was living proof of this love until her death in 1983.

Perhaps no words reflect Corrie's heart of forgiveness and life of love more than these:

> **"My brothers, I want you to know that through Jesus the forgiveness of sins is proclaimed to you."**
> **(Acts 13:38)**

SCRIPTURES TO MEMORIZE

Is my **forgiving** those who **sin against me** and against those I love related to my **heavenly Father's forgiving** my sins?

*"If you **forgive** men when they **sin against you**, your **heavenly Father will also forgive you**. But if you do not forgive men their sins, your Father will not forgive your sins."* (Matthew 6:14–15)

Does God expect me to continue to **forgive** those who repeatedly **sin against me**?

*"Peter came to Jesus and asked, 'Lord, how many times shall I **forgive** my brother when he **sins against me**? Up to seven times?' Jesus answered, 'I tell you, not seven times, but seventy-seven times.'"* (Matthew 18:21–22)

To what degree or in what way am I to be **forgiving of others**?

*"Be kind and compassionate to one another, **forgiving each other**, just as in Christ God forgave you."* (Ephesians 4:32)

Does God expect me to do more than forgive my **enemies** and **those who persecute me**?

*"Love your **enemies** and pray for **those who persecute you**."* (Matthew 5:44)

Are there times when it **promotes love** to not only forgive an offense but to "**cover over an offense**" by not **repeating** it?

*"He who **covers over an offense promotes love**, but whoever **repeats** the matter separates close friends."* (Proverbs 17:9)

Does justice not require that I **take revenge** and **repay evil for evil**?

*"Do not **repay** anyone **evil for evil**. ... Do not **take revenge**, my friends, but leave room for God's wrath, for it is written: 'It is mine to avenge; I will repay,' says the Lord."* (Romans 12:17–19)

Does **being reconciled** to someone who has **something against me** have any effect on my **offering gifts** to God?

*"If you are offering your gift at the altar and there remember that your brother has **something against you**, leave your gift there in front of the altar. First go and **be reconciled** to your brother; then come and **offer your gift**."* (Matt. 5:23–24)

Does God expect me to continue to **bear with those** who sin against me by **forgiving whatever grievances I have against them**?

*"**Bear with each other** and **forgive whatever grievances** you may **have against one another**. Forgive as the Lord forgave you."* (Col. 3:13)

If I should refuse to forgive an offense, will that cause me to **miss the grace of God** in any way or **cause trouble** for me and for others whom I love?

*"See to it that no one **misses the grace of God** and that no bitter root grows up to **cause trouble** and defile many."* (Hebrews 12:15)

NOTES

1. Corrie ten Boom, John L. Sherrill, and Elizabeth Sherrill, *The Hiding Place* (Washington Depot, CT: Chosen, 1971); Corrie ten Boom and Jamie Buckingham, *Tramp for the Lord* (Fort Washington, PA: Christian Literature Crusade, 1974); Corrie ten Boom, *I'm Still Learning to Forgive* (Wheaton, IL: Good News Publishers, 1972), http://www.gnpcb.org/product/663575723080.

2. Ten Boom, *I'm Still Learning to Forgive*, http://www.gnpcb.org/product/663575723080.

3. Robert Jeffress, *When Forgiveness Doesn't Make Sense* (Colorado Springs, CO: WaterBrook, 2000), 47–49.

4. W. E. Vine, *Vine's Complete Expository Dictionary of Biblical Words*, electronic ed., , s.v. "Forgive, Forgave, Forgiveness" (Nashville: Thomas Nelson, 1996).

5. Vine, *Vine's Complete Expository Dictionary*, s.v. "Confess, Confession."

6. Jeffress, *When Forgiveness Doesn't Make Sense,* 46–51.

7. Vine, *Vine's Complete Expository Dictionary*, s.v. "Forgive, Forgave, Forgiveness."

8. For this section see John Nieder and Thomas M. Thompson, *Forgive & Love Again: Healing Wounded Relationships* (Eugene, OR: Harvest House, 1991), 173–85; Jeffress, *When Forgiveness Doesn't Make Sense*, 107–23.

9. Vine, *Vine's Complete Expository Dictionary*, s.v. "Forgive, Forgave, Forgiveness."

10. Vine, *Vine's Complete Expository Dictionary*, s.v. "Grace."

11. Robert Jeffress, *Choose Your Attitudes, Change Your Life* (Wheaton, IL: Victor, 1992), 102–7; see also Chuck Swindoll, "I Am Joseph!" *Insight*, Winter 1986, 3–9.

12. Jeffress, *Choose Your Attitudes, Change Your Life*, 102.

13. Nieder and Thompson, *Forgive & Love Again*, 30.

14. Ten Boom and Buckingham, *Tramp for the Lord*, 54.

15. Nieder and Thompson, *Forgive & Love Again,* 47–51.

16. Lewis B. Smedes, *Forgive and Forget: Healing the Hurts We Don't Deserve* (San Francisco, CA: Harper & Row, 1984), 138–41.

17. David A. Stoop, *Real Solutions for Forgiving the Unforgivable*, Real Solutions Series (Ann Arbor, MI: Vine, 2001), 69–82.

18. J. C. Grider, "Forgiveness," in *Evangelical Dictionary of Theology,* ed. Walter A. Elwell, 2nd ed., Baker Reference Library (Grand Rapids: Baker Academic, 2001), 460.

19. Lawrence J. Crabb, Jr., *Understanding People: Deep Longings for Relationship*, Ministry Resources Library (Grand Rapids: Zondervan, 1987), 15–16; Robert S. McGee, *The Search for Significance*, 2nd ed. (Houston, TX: Rapha, 1990), 27–30.

20. Ten Boom and Buckingham, *Tramp for the Lord*, 181.

21. Nieder and Thompson, *Forgive & Love Again*, 51–56.

22. David Augsburger, *The Freedom of Forgiveness*, rev. and exp. ed. (Chicago: Moody, 1988), 18.

23. Augsburger, *The Freedom of Forgiveness*, 47–50.

24. Smedes, *Forgive and Forget*, 21–26.

25. Smedes, *Forgive and Forget*, 23.

26. Augsburger, *The Freedom of Forgiveness*, 44–46.

27. Smedes, *Forgive and Forget*, 31–37.

28. Augsburger, *The Freedom of Forgiveness*, 42; Smedes, *Forgive and Forget*, 111–13.

29. Vine, *Vine's Complete Expository Dictionary*, s.v. "Love."

30. Bill Gothard, *Basic Seminar Textbook: Research in Principles of Life* (Oak Brook, IL: Institute in Basic Life Principles, 1981), Used by permission.

31. Ten Boom, Sherrill, and Sherrill, *The Hiding Place*, 238.

SELECTED BIBLIOGRAPHY

Augsburger, David. *The Freedom of Forgiveness*. Rev. and exp. ed. Chicago: Moody, 1988.

Crabb, Lawrence J., Jr. *Understanding People: Deep Longings for Relationship*. Ministry Resources Library. Grand Rapids: Zondervan, 1987.

Grider, J. C. "Forgiveness." In *Evangelical Dictionary of Theology*, edited by Walter A. Elwell. 2nd ed., 460. Baker Reference Library. Grand Rapids: Baker Academic, 2001.

Hunt, June. *Counseling Through Your Bible Handbook*. Eugene, Oregon: Harvest House Publishers, 2007.

Hunt, June. *How to Forgive . . . When You Don't Feel Like It*. Eugene, Oregon: Harvest House Publishers, 2007.

Hunt, June. *How to Handle Your Emotions*. Eugene, Oregon: Harvest House Publishers, 2008.

Hunt, June. *Seeing Yourself Through God's Eyes*. Eugene, Oregon: Harvest House Publishers, 2008

Jeffress, Robert. *Choose Your Attitudes, Change Your Life*. Wheaton, IL: Victor, 1992.

Jeffress, Robert. *When Forgiveness Doesn't Make Sense*. Colorado Springs, CO: WaterBrook, 2000.

McGee, Robert S. *The Search for Significance*. 2nd ed. Houston, TX: Rapha, 1990.

Nieder, John, and Thomas M. Thompson. *Forgive & Love Again: Healing Wounded Relationships.* Eugene, OR: Harvest House, 1991.

Smedes, Lewis B. *The Art of Forgiving: When You Need to Forgive and Don't Know How.* New York: Ballantine, 1997.

Smedes, Lewis B. *Forgive and Forget: Healing the Hurts We Don't Deserve.* San Francisco, CA: Harper & Row, 1984.

Stoop, David A. *Real Solutions for Forgiving the Unforgivable.* Real Solutions Series. Ann Arbor, MI: Vine, 2001.

Swindoll, Chuck. "I Am Joseph!" *Insight*, Winter 1986, 3–9.

Ten Boom, Corrie. *I'm Still Learning to Forgive.* Wheaton, IL: Good News Publishers, 1972. http://www.gnpcb.org/product/663575723080.

Ten Boom, Corrie, and Jamie Buckingham. *Tramp for the Lord.* Fort Washington, PA: Christian Literature Crusade, 1974.

Ten Boom, Corrie, John L. Sherrill, and Elizabeth Sherrill. *The Hiding Place.* Washington Depot, CT: Chosen, 1971.

June Hunt's HOPE FOR THE HEART booklets are biblically-based, and full of practical advice that is relevant, spiritually-fulfilling and wholesome. Each topic presents scriptural truths and examples of real-life situations to help readers relate and integrate June's counseling guidance into their own lives. Practical for individuals from all walks of life, this new booklet series invites readers into invaluable restoration, emotional health, and spiritual freedom.

HOPE FOR THE HEART TITLES

www.aspirepress.com

The HOPE FOR THE HEART Biblical Counseling Library is Your Solution!

- Easy-to-read, perfect for anyone.
- Short. Only 92 pages. Good for the busy person.
- Christ-centered biblical advice and practical help
- Tested and proven over 20 years of June Hunt's radio ministry
- 25 titles in the series – each tackling a key issue people face today.
- Affordable. You or your church can give away, lend, or sell them.

Display available for churches and ministries.

www.aspirepress.com